The World Behind Her Eyes

Eliza Klaski

BookLeaf Publishing

India | USA | UK

Presentation by *BookLeaf Publishing*

Web: www.bookleafpub.com

E-mail: info@bookleafpub.com

ISBN: 9789358313680

First edition 2024

I do not have hurt.

You cannot tell me that I do not have hurt, until you have crawled inside my mind and spent a night in the confusion, until you have walked down the dimly lit steps leading to my heart, and witnessed her body being racked with sobs, gasping for air on the floor of her room. You cannot tell me that I do not have hurt unless you dare to take my grief by the hand, look her in the eyes and say that to her face.

Sour(Sorrow) Water

Out of the overflow of the heart the mouth speaks, but how can her words be anything but sadness when sorrow is the only water that pours from her tap?

Blue waters.

3

The blue of your eyes ran like water to the floor
and I can't help but hate myself because I know
that I am the reason it's for.

I hate weed.

My body is mine to give, not yours to take.
Countless people have desired it, few have
gotten a taste, still others, angry by my refusal,
tried to steal it.
I am not a thing to be passed around, a toy for
your entertainment.
Used. Discarded, like one of the blunts you had
so desperately wanted me to hit.

What is the point of life?

5

But I wonder if that isn't the point of life...to love and to be loved.

Ocean Eyes

I never was a fan of blue eyes until I recognized
the ocean I so love inside of yours.

Sharing rooms.

I always hated having to share a room with you,
but god I would give the whole world to have
just one more sleepover.

I wish you knew how sorry I am.

Your heart is shattered on the floor and it's all my fault. It got caught in the crossfire of my confusion and trauma and there's not a single thing that I could do to undo the damage that has been done. I wish I could make it right. I'm falling apart at the seams and the one thing I wish you knew is how very sorry I am.

Until the sunrise.

I am tired, my darling. Would you lay with me a while? Would you hold me until the sun rises and we can redo today, tomorrow?

Speechless Polyglot

And sometimes, I keep my feelings to myself,
for I can find no language to describe them in.

A lake can never love you like the sea.

The sea is only place I have ever felt truly seen, truly known. No religious structure has ever for me created such an environment of safety and peace the way she has.

In her I could paddle away from the reality of my life until my lungs gasped for air and my bones could no longer pull me forward.

I could sit in the cool embrace of the deep waters and allow myself to believe that these things would soon pass.

That I would make it through them.

Now I live in a sea-less place and wonder if I ever knew anything at all.

frozen & rotting

I am scared that I will never go anywhere in life.
I am scared that I have spent all of my adventure
too early, and I will be sentenced to monotony
and melancholy for the rest of my days.
This fear paralyzes me. I cannot move forward. I
cannot breathe. I cannot dream.
I dare not hope.
I cannot risk my life being something I hate, but
simultaneously, I cannot leave this place.
I fear I will spend my life rotting in this hell
hole.

Aesthete

Fight against me all that you want.
Beat me until I'm black and blue.
Tell me that you never cared for me.
It will never stop me from seeing the beauty in
you.

I am an unknown dialect.

I once cried and all I wanted was my mom to say
something, anything, even if she didn't know
what to say.
She just looked at me.
I felt like an alien.
Like no one could ever understand me.
Like I was written in a language foreign to the
whole world.

Jealousy.

I am jealous.
Jealous of the lone star in the sky.
She is safe. She is loved. She has purpose.
I am not like the lone star in the sky.
Rather, I stand here on Earth,
jealous of the lone star in the sky.

The embrace of being unknown.

I cannot remember the last time an embrace caused me to feel safe and not like a response to something the one embracing me simply had no words for.

Naiveté

A thousand blows to my heart have not stopped me from believing your lies, and I fear the same outcome after a thousand more.

The comfort of kitchens.

I think that my kitchen floor has caught more tears than any grave ever has.

Raising myself.

I want my father to hold me, but I don't want
him to touch me.
I want my mother to console me, but I fear she
will only judge me.
I want my parents to be my parents, but it feels
like so long since I've relieved them of that duty
that I'm not sure I want that anymore.

Drown me.

Drown me in your ocean.
Drown me in the ocean that is your eyes.

Suicide & Stolen Art

The way people look at me makes me wonder if I am not alive, but am a long forgotten piece of art, stolen from time.

9 789358 313680